30 DAYS OF FUN READING ACTIVITIES

BUILDING READING SKILLS IN RELUCTANT READERS

K KODAK

INTRODUCTION

For some learners reading is no fun. And it's hard to learn or improve when you aren't having fun.

This book offers 30 fun ways to practice reading -- one for every day of the month!

With each activity you will be practicing core reading skills such as inferencing, prediction, main idea, description, etc, AND you and your learner will be having a great time!

Get started on the first activity today. Turn reading into fun!

Activity 1

Write a Story

Ask your learner to tell you a story.

If your learner has trouble, use questions to help your learner figure out the parts of their story.

Characters: Who is this story about?

Setting: Where does this story take place?

Genre: Is the story a mystery? Is it a true story? etc.

If you can, write or type the story as your child tells it to you. Keep the story going by asking questions to lead your child into new thoughts.

Enjoy your child's imagination!

At the end, read the story back to your learner, or even better, ask your child to read it to you.

Quickly draw four pictures that represent some of the activities done recently — stick figures are fine!

Next get your child to write a few sentences about each picture. Use the words 'WHO, WHEN, WHERE, DOING WHAT, WHY, FEELINGS' to give ideas about what to write.

Aim for 2-4 sentences per picture. If your child is enthusiastic, let them write as much as they want.

After each picture, have your child read what they have written to you or to another adult.

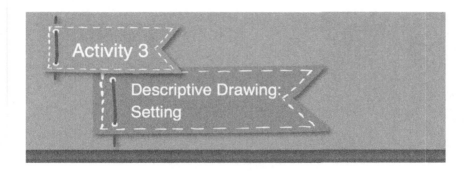

Find a paragraph that describes the setting of a story (where or when it happened.) The paragraph can be from a familiar or unfamiliar book.

Read the paragraph aloud and ask your learner to draw a picture of what they heard.

Read it again to see if they can add more details to their drawing. Stop when you feel they have included the majority of the details.

The first time you do this; choose a paragraph with concrete details like specific shapes, colors, locations, etc.

As your child improves you can choose books with more sophisticated descriptions.

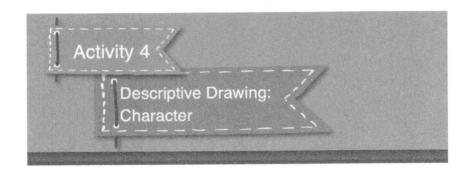

Find a paragraph that describes a character. Read the paragraph aloud and ask your reader to draw a picture of what they heard.

Read the paragraph again to see if they can add more details to their drawing. Stop when you feel they have included the majority of the details.

For this activity, it is important to select a paragraph that describes the character clearly.

Activity 5

Creating a Junk Mail Dictionary

Today your learner makes a fun dictionary.

Cut out pictures of six different objects from junk mail flyers and paste each on a separate piece of paper.

Have your child write one word that describes each picture. Next, ask your child to write what the word means and a complete sentence using that word. Underline the word in that sentence.

Advanced: If the word has other age-appropriate meanings, think about them and add them at the bottom. e.g. 'boot' can be footwear or but it can also be an action.

Activity 6

Treasure Hunt

Using the following six clues, set up a simple treasure hunt in your home. Think of a small reward for your learner to find at the end of the hunt.

Hide all the clues except for the first in the location specified by the previous clue. Give the first clue to your reader to begin the hunt. Allow your leaner to read each clue for themselves, unless they need a little help.

Clue #1

Let the fun begin! Go to the place where dishes become clean and look inside.

Clue #2

I am comfortable and soft and your head spends a lot of time on me at night. Look under me.

. . .

Clue #3

You are halfway there, only a few more clues until you find your treasure! Sometimes we need to clean ourselves. Go to the place where you get wet and soapy at the same time.

Clue #4

When your family gets hungry, everyone goes here to enjoy a meal together. Go to your spot and look underneath.

Clue #5

Only one more clue to find and you will receive your reward! Go to the place where clothes are made clean. There is something hidden down below.

Clue #6

You've worked hard to make it this far. You will find your prize hidden near your favorite shoes.

Print out an interesting news story that might interest your reader and cut the paragraphs apart.

Place the paragraphs in a bowl and mix them up. Ask your child to read the paragraphs and put them in the right order.

Today your learner is going to be a character detective.

Find an easy-to-read fiction book that might appeal to your learner. It can also be a book they are already familiar with.

Make a chart for your learner to fill in similar to the following. The categories will depend on the character/book you have chosen.

Ask your learner to search for the information to fill in the chart.

Name:

Age:

Hair color:

Family members:

Likes:

Dislikes:

Activity 9

Make a Menu

Today your learner writes their own menu.

First help your learner decide what kind of restaurant the menu is for. Let them think of items to include and ways to describe the food.

Encourage your learner to go beyond simple descriptions like "peanut butter and jelly sandwich." Support them in developing fun descriptions like "crunchy peanut butter and wild raspberry jam served on country white bread with or without the crusts."

You can extend this activity by searching for (and reading!) a recipe to make one of the dishes.

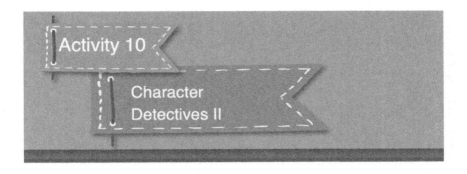

Activity 10

Character Detectives II

Your learner is going to do some more detective work today.

Find an easy-to-read book and look through it for a minor character that appears somewhere towards the front of the book.

Make some clues for your learner to guess which character it is. For example:

- This character is wearing a blue shirt.
- This character buys something from a shop.
- This character gets mad.

Read through the clues with your learner and then ask them to find out which character it is.

Activity 11

All About The Cover

In this activity, your child will create a new cover for their favorite book, story or movie.

Using any books you have available, talk about what is included on the front and back covers, such as an image, the title of the book, the author and illustrator's name, etc.

Next, cover a cereal box (or something similar) with white paper. Now it is time for your child to create their front and back cover for their favorite book, story or movie.

Help them refer to the sample books if they need help remembering what to include.

As a last step, get your learner to explain his/her book cover to you or another interested adult.

Activity 12

Teacher For A Day!

Today your child is the teacher and you will answer the questions!

Choose an age-appropriate reading book. Non-fiction may work best.

Have your child read a paragraph aloud from the book (or 1-2 sentences, if that is easier). Next, they ask you a question based on what they read. For example, the sentence "Butterflies have four wings." could lead to the question "How many wings does a butterfly have?"

Encourage your child to ask 'Who', 'What', 'Why', 'How many', and 'Where' questions.

Sometimes give the wrong answer and make sure your child corrects you!

Activity 13

Scavenger Hunt!

It's time for a scavenger hunt.

Make a list of 5-10 people, items or events mentioned in one of your learner's favorite books. It should be a book they have read or are familiar with.

Give your learner the list and the book. Their task is to find where each item is mentioned and note down the page number.

Provide a reward for finding every item on the list!

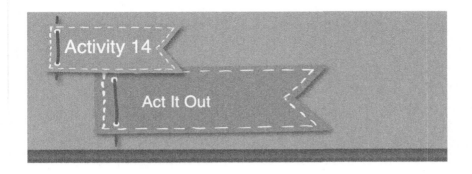

Find a short story or favourite scene from a book.

Read the scene together and then act it out. Bring in other members of the family if you want to make it a family event.

You may even want to video your performance for grandma or a special aunt.

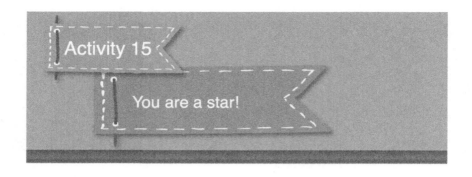

Choose a book and record your child reading aloud. Let them listen to it.

Talk about what was good and what was challenging. Make some suggestions on how it might sound better.

Record them again, and praise them for every improvement they make!

In this activity, your learner is a reporter whose job is to write an article about a favourite pet or stuffed animal.

You will be the voice of the pet/stuffed animal. Your learner asks you questions so that they have information to write about.

For younger learners, help them brainstorm a list of questions.

After the interview, your learner writes an article based on the information they learned.

If needed, you can model the process first by being the newspaper reporter.

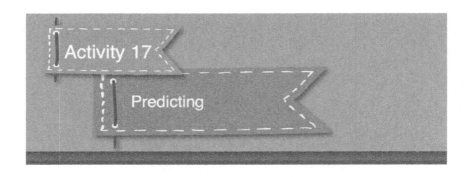

Activity 17

Predicting

In this activity your child practices making predictions about what might happen next.

You will need: a fiction book your child has never read before. You can read the pages to your child or they can read it themselves.

Read the first paragraph or page (depending on your learner). Stop and ask questions like: what do you think will happen next? What is the most likely thing to happen? Name one or two things that could possibly happen.

Read on to see if you were right, and then talk about it.

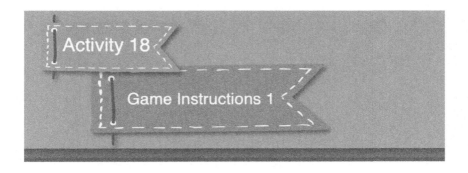

Activity 18

Game Instructions 1

In today's activities, you scan and extract information from board game instructions.

You will need: instructions from some easy board or card games. If you don't own any, you can find some online.

Choose one of the instructions and read it through together. Ask your learner questions such as: How many people can play? How do you set up the game? How does a player win? What items are needed to play the game?

Choose the questions based on the comprehension skills of your learner. Make sure you model how you are finding the information: "Look, the title of this section is 'How to Win'. It will tell us what to do to win."

Next, repeat the task with the instructions from another game and see if your learner can answer some of the same questions independently. If not, do it together again. All this practice is developing your child's reading skills.

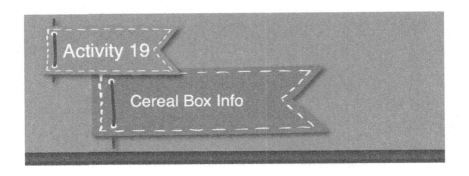

Activity 19

Cereal Box Info

In today's activity, your reading material will be cereal boxes!

You will need: several boxes of breakfast cereal, or similar.

Choose one of the boxes and read the information on the outside of the box together.

Depending on the level of your reader you might stay with simple information like the name of the cereal and identifying who makes it. More advanced learners could be introduced to the nutrition and ingredient information.

After looking at one box together, hand a second box to your child and ask them to tell you some information about it. If they struggle, model the process again by doing it together. It's all learning!

Activity 20

Cookie Recipes

You will need: some kid friendly cookie recipes.

Choose one of the recipes and read it together, explaining the different parts of the recipe, such as the ingredient list, the instructions, etc. Limit your explanation to what is suitable for your child... you may not want to explain the whole measuring system to a Kindergarten learner!

Next, ask questions about the recipe, such as: how many cookies will the recipe make? What temperature for the oven? Help your child find the answer. Get them to ask you some questions, too!

Pass a second recipe to your child and ask similar questions. If they need help, do it together or reverse roles.

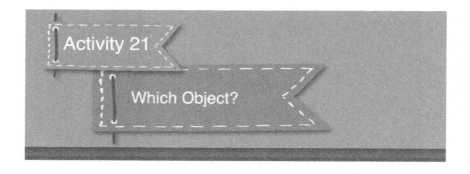

Activity 21

Which Object?

In this activity your child practices describing objects.

WHAT YOU'LL NEED:

- About six objects of different colors, shapes and sizes. The more similar the objects are, the more challenging the activity will be.
- Paper
- Pen or pencil

HERE'S HOW TO DO IT:

Place the objects in the middle of a table. Choose one of them and describe it to your child without saying what it is. Explain the importance of including the details that make it different from the others. Have your child help you describe it. Remove that object from the pile.

Next, your child chooses one of the other objects and writes a description (without using its name). When they're done writing the description have them read it out loud and you guess which object they wrote about.

Now reverse the task. You write a description of an object and your child reads the description and figure outs which object you described.

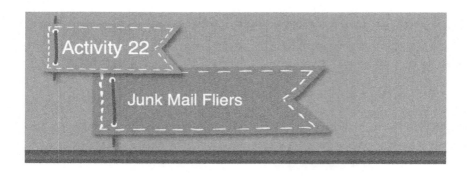

You will need: 3-4 advertising fliers.

Browse through one of the fliers with your child, talking aloud about the information you see, such as the price, description, reviews, etc.

Next get a different flier and find the information together.

Finally, ask your child to browse the flier and find something to tell you about. Prompt with questions if needed.

You will need: 3-4 advertising fliers, ideally advertising multiple items.

Read one of the fliers and identify one advertised item that you would like and explain why. Then choose one you would never want and explain why.

Now it is your child's turn. If needed, help them with the explanation of why they want/don't want a specific item.

Print out a text that should appeal to your reader such as a joke, a brochure for Disney World, a favourite story, etc.

Next, take a black marker and coverup one or two words from each sentence.

Your learner's task is to fill in the missing words. They can choose words that are silly or realistic, as long as the sentence reads like an English sentence.

When the blanks are filled, get your learner to read their new text.

Activity 25

Spot the Difference

Today's activity helps build focus and attention as well as reading skills.

Read a sentence/paragraph/page aloud to your learner, but change something significant when you read. (Don't make it obvious and don't let your reader see the page as you are reading).

Next, get your learner to read the same section and see if they can find what is different from your version.

Let them re-read the section again if they want. You can repeat your version again, too.

If your child has trouble, narrow down to the one sentence/paragraph with the change.

Activity 26

Newspaper Scavenger Hunt

A newspaper scavenger hunt is a great way for your reader to learn how to *skim* for information.

Browse a local newspaper and come up with 5-10 targets for your scavenger hunt. Some examples are:

- What page does the sports section start on?
- Find an article that is about a cat.
- What page has the crossword?
- Find an article about another country.
- Is there are recipe in the paper?

Today your learner is a playwright!

With your learner, brainstorm some ideas for a play for your family to act in. Make it as crazy and silly as you like.

Next, get your learner to write out the parts.

Once the play is written, give each family member his or her part to read, and put on a show in your living room.

Pull a Story Out of a Hat!

Today your learner makes up silly stories.

Take several strips of paper and write silly sentences on them. For example, one could read "I tripped on a snail." Another could say "Tomorrow, I will ride on a frog!"

Take all of the strips of paper and toss them together in a bowl.

Have your child pull the strips out, one at a time, and read them aloud.

After reading the silly sentence, ask your learner to make up a silly story to go with it.

If your learner likes to write, let them choose their favorite made-up story and write it out.

Activity 29

Thank-You Letter

Writing activities have reading built in to them so they are always a good choice for a reluctant reader.

Today, have your child write a letter to someone who has given them something or done something nice for them recently. It may even be a letter to you!

After they have written the letter, get them to read it to you.

In this activity, your learner creates a mental image based on a paragraph you read.

Creating mental images helps readers better understand and retain what they are reading.

Read aloud a descriptive or action-packed paragraph from a book. Ask your child to close their eyes and create a mental image or movie while you read.

Remind your learner to try and include the five senses in their mental image: sight, sound, smell, taste and touch. This makes for a richer, more memorable image.

At the end, your learner draws their image, or describes it to you.

BEFORE YOU GO

I hope you had fun with the activities in this book.

For more practice, start back at the beginning and repeat! Your learner will approach the activities with more confidence and you will be impressed with how far he/she has progressed in 30 days.

Have fun on the journey while you help your child learn to read!

Printed in Great Britain
by Amazon

84511574R00031